MORAL EDUCATION
AND THE CURRICULUM

MORAL EDUCATION AND THE CURRICULUM

A guide for teachers and research workers

BY

JOHN WILSON

Director of the Farmington
Trust Research Unit

THE QUEEN'S AWARD
TO INDUSTRY 1966

PERGAMON PRESS

OXFORD · LONDON · EDINBURGH · NEW YORK
TORONTO · SYDNEY · PARIS · BRAUNSCHWEIG

Pergamon Press Ltd., Headington Hill Hall, Oxford
4 & 5 Fitzroy Square, London W.1
Pergamon Press (Scotland) Ltd., 2 & 3 Teviot Place, Edinburgh 1
Pergamon Press Inc., Maxwell House, Fairview Park, Elmsford, New York 10523
Pergamon of Canada Ltd., 207 Queen's Quay West, Toronto 1
Pergamon Press (Aust.) Pty. Ltd., 19a Boundary Street, Rushcutters Bay, N.S.W. 2011, Australia
Pergamon Press S.A.R.L., 24 rue des Écoles, Paris 5ᵉ
Vieweg & Sohn GmbH, Burgplatz 1, Braunschweig

Copyright © 1969 Farmington Trust Ltd.
First edition 1969
Library of Congress Catalog Card No. 72–78 592

Printed in Great Britain by Hazell Watson & Viney Ltd., Aylesbury, Bucks

08 013898 5 (flexicover)
08 013897 7 (hard cover)

Contents

Preface

EDUCATIONAL thought proceeds always in two dimensions, the theoretical and the practical. Progress is sometimes made in consequence of a new theory, developed perhaps from psychological experiment, as happened over the notion of the transfer of training: sometimes in consequence of random experiment in the classroom, as happened over the introduction of "creative writing". It is plain, however, that significant progress relies on an interplay between theory and practice. Innovations in the classroom, if they work at all, are facts which the theorist must take into account: innovations in theory have to be tested in the classroom, and perhaps corrected in the light of the facts that then emerge.

The pages that follow relate partly to some preliminary work in the aims and theory of moral education, which has already been published.[1] But we are here concerned neither to go further in the realms of theory nor to make definite recommendations about the practical measures to be taken. What we offer here is a guide for research on the topic, which teachers and others are invited to use in conjunction with their own experience and reflections. The guide will, we hope, be of practical value not only to teachers, but also to education authorities, research workers in colleges of education, and others who may have neither the time, money nor energy to conduct large-scale research programmes, and who yet wish to gain a somewhat clearer view of school practice in respect to moral education. I take this to be a sufficient justification for the enterprise: whether this guide does the job well the reader must judge for himself.

I am grateful to the Schools Council in particular for producing a situation in which the need for this particular guide became obvious. The Council's curricular research and development project on moral education, based at the Institute of Education of Oxford University, has been working closely with us since it started in September of 1967. A large part of its task was to take a look at school practice in the local area, and to encourage teachers to do the same. Some means of doing this coherently, and of making some kind of assessment (however rough), was urgently needed. Out of that need this guide was conceived: and I am grateful not only to the Schools Council, but to all those who have (unwittingly) administered that particular type of swift kick in the psychological pants which reminds us that our research is supposed to be (as the jargon goes) operational, and not merely theoretical: especially to Harold Loukes and Alec Peterson.

Oxford, 1968   J.B.W.

[1] *Introduction to Moral Education*, by John Wilson, Norman Williams and Barry Sugarman (Penguin Books, 1968).

Introduction

In this Unit's first publication[1] we argued for a particular concept of a "morally educated person", which was outlined in terms of a set of "moral components".[2] It is the aim of moral education, as also of any similar enterprise which may be differently named ("human relations", "learning to live", etc.), to develop all these components in children and adolescents.

In order to discover, with even a weak claim at all to certainty, what factors in schools and other institutions actually promote the development of these moral components, we first need to develop adequate methods of testing and assessment:[3] and this is the task on which this Unit is currently engaged. This is likely to take some time, and it is far from clear what degree of success we can expect in the vast enterprise of devising a battery of tests and other methods of verification. But it does not follow from this that no useful investigation or research can be done in the meantime: and in particular it is likely that headmasters, inspectors of schools, research workers in colleges of education, local authorities and many others will want to take a look at schools and other educational institutions, to see how far what they are doing is likely to be profitable for the moral education of their pupils. This guide is an attempt to meet this need.

One thing, however, must be made clear from the start. Those who will use this guide will, no doubt, be interested not only in an analysis of what actually goes on in schools: they will also want to take action on this basis—perhaps to devise new curricula and new teaching methods. It would be wholly wrong for this Unit actually to recommend what changes should be made: such recommendations must be deferred until our long-term research is completed. But there should be nothing to deter (and a good deal to encourage) those who will use this guide, if they are themselves responsible for school practice, from making their own recommendations on the basis of their own assessment. By describing briefly how this would occur, we may also be able to give the reader some idea of how the guide is to be used.

A. The Plan of the Guide

1. First, we shall try in the following section to get clear about how the curriculum ties in and overlaps with other features of the school. This is necessary in order to make sure that we know what we shall be talking about in the rest of the book.
2. In Chapter 1, we shall begin by speaking briefly of methods of assessment, and go on to spell out the moral components (in terms of which the assessments are to be made) in more detail. We shall try to show how these components may be observed in children and adolescents. These represent the aims of moral education, and it is to these that the curricular practices which we are investigating must be referred. We shall also say something about other possible aims in which the investigator may be interested.
3. In Chapter 2, we come to the main point of this guide. We shall there offer an analytic model for the curriculum: that is, a way of looking at what is taught and how, and of asking the right questions about it. By answering the questions given in the model, and comparing them with his assessment in terms of the moral components, the investigator will be able to get a clearer and more detailed picture both of what actually goes on in the school curriculum, and of what features in it seem to contribute towards moral education. Finally, we shall suggest some further questions that may be of particular interest to those investigators who are concerned with taking some practical action for the improvement and reform of the curriculum.

All this will, of course, seem much over-simplified. In particular the assessment (very briefly discussed in Chapter 1) is bound to be difficult, for lack of ade-

---

[1] *Introduction to Moral Education*, by John Wilson, Norman Williams and Barry Sugarman (Penguin Books, January 1968): referred to below as *I.M.E.*
[2] *I.M.E.*, pp. 192 *et seq.*   [3] *I.M.E.*, pp. 117 *et seq.*

quate instruments. Nevertheless, it seems to us quite likely that teachers and others will be able to have a fairly clear idea, after using the analytical models, of some factors at least which seem to be beneficial for moral education. If and when they have such a clear idea, they will be able to consider how these factors should be built into the school practice: and subsequently they will be able to investigate the new practices in their turn and make some assessment of them.

B. The Curriculum and Other Features

In this guide we have separated off one feature of school life, "the curriculum", from other features which may be equally or more important for moral education. The obvious advantage of this is that it gives the investigator a narrower area to work in, and one which he can analyse in more detail. But the difficulty about it is that many non-curricular features in a school may be relevant to moral education, and some obviously are. This guide will have done harm rather than good if it is assumed that the whole (or even the chief) effort of a school which wants to improve its moral education should be devoted to providing one or two new periods in the curriculum. Certainly this is one of the easiest ways to think about moral education; but equally certainly it is one of the most superficial.

A forthcoming publication of the Unit[1] attempts to give a more general picture of the school as a social institution, and incorporates a good many more features; but it should be easy to see the importance of two other general classes of features besides the curriculum—the social context, and the personality of the teacher. We need to realise here that the distinctions between (1) the curriculum, (2) the social context, and (3) the personality of the teacher are to a great extent artificial. It is necessary to understand how they may in practice overlap, otherwise the investigator may miss out factors of great importance. This overlap is very obvious if we consider (3), the personality of the teacher. Teachers do not affect their pupils in isolation: they affect them *in* teaching subjects of the curriculum, or *in* the wider social context of the school.

Similarly the distinction between (1) and (2) is very artificial. For, first, when a pupil learns a subject he *also* has certain social experiences (he is sitting in a class with other pupils, is expected not to talk while the lesson is going on, and so forth): so that our subject-teaching will also play an important part in

[1] By Dr. Barry Sugarman, *The School, Socialization and Moral Education.*

the social context. And secondly, teachers may (and no doubt ought to) so arrange particular social contexts in the school that the pupils do in fact *learn* from them: what they learn may not be exactly a subject or a topic—it may be more like a particular social skill, such as how to behave on a school outing or when being entertained to tea—but they are intended to learn something. So in a way many of the "social experiences" in (2) *could* in principle form part of a curriculum. For instance, we could have a subject called "learning about other people's feelings", and teach it by having tea-parties, discussions, games and school outings: if we had these at regular times and intervals, it could go into the time-table.

As long as we bear this firmly in mind, however, the distinction which we are making may still be a useful one for the practical purposes of this guide. For it is a very open question just how much time a school should spend in subjecting its pupils to anything that might reasonably be called a *curriculum*, as opposed to leaving them free to have certain experiences which are not controlled and organised so tightly by the teacher as to count as a *subject*. Thus we might think that we ought to have a subject or topic taught for two periods every week called "getting on with your classmates": but we might also think that we should leave the children free actually to get on with their classmates, and learn what they can from the simple experience of being with them—and this would be a matter of social experience rather than a curricular subject. (Of course we might think that we should do both.)

This point is very relevant to any recommendations that may be based on the investigations suggested in this guide. Those who are responsible for the running of a school will have to answer at least one important question in the first place, if they are to make proper use of this book. They will have to decide whether in fact the school deals with something under the heading of "curriculum" or "social context"—whether it sets out actually to *teach* it, or whether it leaves it for the pupils to learn from their social experiences. For instance, many schools will perhaps feel that the areas generally labelled "sex" and "citizenship" are areas in which pupils should, somehow, be educated. Some will deliberately set out to teach their pupils *about* sex (perhaps in biology classes) and "citizenship" (perhaps in discussions): others may feel that these are best left to the free experiences of the child, both at school and elsewhere, or should be dealt with entirely outside the school.

At the analytic stage, the investigator will be concerned only with what actually does go on under these headings. But any headmaster or other authority, in considering what his school actually does, will be led to consider how far he thinks it is right in doing what it does. So he will need to ask himself first of all whether the things which he wants his pupils to learn are in fact being dealt with *under the right headings*: that is, whether a certain area which now forms part of the curriculum might not in fact be better served by leaving it to the free social experience of the pupil, or conversely whether an area which is not now in the curriculum might not profit-ably be incorporated in it. The point here is that he cannot abdicate responsibility for this decision: if he thinks, for instance, that "getting on with one's classmates" or "sex" are areas which cannot well be taught in the curriculum, and that the pupils will learn them well enough if they are left to their own devices in the school, he must have some grounds for believing that the pupils actually *will* learn them well enough in this way. He cannot just *hope*. A decision *not* to teach something in curricular form is just as important as a decision *to* teach it.

CHAPTER 1

Assessment and the Moral Components

A. Assessment

What we offer here is a method of assessment that falls short of the rigour and precision of strict psychological testing, but which is more formally structured than intuitive judgement. There are very few good tests or questionnaires which are demonstrably relevant to the moral components, if indeed there are any at all: and we do not expect that many investigators will have time or resources to apply many tests of this kind. If an investigator does wish to use these methods, he should take expert advice. On the other hand, he should be able to do more than merely use his intuition. But the investigator must rely largely on his own judgement about methods of assessment, since the methods he uses will in any case depend on how he is placed as regards the particular school he is investigating.

SOURCES OF ASSESSMENT

1. *Teachers.* Plainly the opinion of those who teach the pupils in school is important: particularly perhaps of those whose job it is to know something about the pupils as people (rather than only as academic performers—a pupil's housemaster or tutor, for example).
2. *Own observation.* The investigator himself will be able to observe, or may already have observed, the pupils' behaviour in the school and outside.
3. *Outside contacts.* The pupil's parents, the leader of his youth club (if any), and anyone else in a position to give information may be useful sources.
4. *Pupil's friends.* The pupil's contemporaries—friends in his class or gang, etc.—may give useful information.
5. *Interviews and informal discussion.* By talking with the pupils, either in the form of a struc-

tured interview (which follows some regular pattern, and in which the same or similar questions are asked) or more informally, the investigator may come to see how they think and feel.
6. *Pupil's written evidence.* Whilst the investigator may not feel able to draw up specific questionnaires (not at least without taking expert advice first), he may gain useful information from pupil's written essays about moral problems, or about situations involving other people.

We cannot here consider the vast topic of the merits and demerits of these methods: those who wish to pursue this topic may like to consult the relevant works of reference. But some of the more obvious dangers may be mentioned.

1. *Beliefs induced by the investigation itself.* Teachers and others may be too apt to believe that curricular periods, or social features of the school, do in fact succeed in realising their aims —particularly if they have been deliberately devised for that purpose. Thus if, for example, a school sets out specifically to teach "awareness" in classroom periods, in a course lasting a whole year, it requires some courage to admit at the end (after analysis and assessment) that the pupils have not in fact developed their "awareness" at all: yet this may well be the case.
2. *Prejudices of observers.* This danger is very obvious in the case of pupils' parents, but may also apply to their teachers and other associates. The investigator must do his best to note and discount the prejudices and personal moral judgements of those to whom he goes for information.
3. *Pupil's expectations.* Material that comes from the pupils themselves (in interviews, informal talks or written essays) may be vitiated not (or not only) by active dishonesty or lying, but rather by the pupils' desire to give the investigator the sort of answers they think he wants—

1

probably those which the pupils regard as "moral" or "respectable" answers.

4. *Effect of observer on observed.* In many educational experiments it has been found that the process of observation itself, and the general concern of the investigator, has a pronounced effect on the pupils observed. This is not so much a matter of the pupils trying to satisfy the observer, as in (3) above, but a matter of the increased stimulation of, and attention paid to, the pupils. So far as possible, the investigator should try to avoid this or to allow for it.

The best way for the investigator to get clear about what sort of questions he wants to ask (and have answered) is for him *first* to get clear about the nature of each of the components. If he is really sure about what is *meant* by PHIL, EMP, etc., he will then himself see what kinds of questions naturally and logically follow in each case. What we shall do, then, is to list and describe the moral components, and add a selection of questions that the investigator might wish to use. It must of course be recognised that both the description of the components, and the questions suggested, are by no means ideally complete or sufficiently detailed: but they may serve our present purpose well enough.

B. The Moral Components

PHIL

What is PHIL?

PHIL is an *attitude* or a frame of mind: it is not simply an ability or a piece of knowledge. Various ways of describing this attitude might be "regarding other people as equals", "thinking that other people's interests count", "weighing other people's interests equally with one's own", "looking on other people as human beings with rights", "taking notice of other people's wants and needs", "not thinking that one's own interests are a special case", "having a concern for their interests", and so on.

1. Attitudes like PHIL are detected and verified by the way in which a person thinks in his everyday, practical living, and to some extent by the way in which he acts. We must be careful here, however, because it is possible for a person to have this attitude but not to act on it—perhaps because he does not know how to, or because he is frightened, or for some other reason: and failures of this kind would be failures of KRAT, not of PHIL.[1] However, the person

[1] See below under KRAT.

must to *some* extent act up to his attitude: in the extreme case, if he never did so, we should rightly doubt whether he really had that attitude. In this respect PHIL differs from EMP and GIG:[2] EMP and GIG are respectively an ability and an attainment, and a person may have these without ever actually using them in his everyday life. PHIL, on the other hand, must to some extent be detectable in a person's practical living.

2. On the cognitive side, PHIL involves a *belief*—the belief that other people have equal rights with oneself. (This is related to (1) above: if beliefs are genuine, they to some extent show themselves in action.) This belief should normally go along with an emotion or *feeling*—that of respect for, or caring about, other people—and the two merge into an attitude adopted towards them. We have to beware, however, of misinterpreting PHIL in two ways:

(a) By regarding it as *only* a matter of belief: i.e. as long as the person *says* he believes in the equality of other people's interests, that is sufficient. The danger of this can be shown by considering the example of a person who says (and perhaps in some sense really thinks) that he is not prejudiced against negroes and regards them as equals, but who in his feelings and behaviour shows quite clearly that he is.

(b) By regarding some *intense* feeling (e.g. of brotherhood, love, strong sympathy, identification with, etc.) as necessary for PHIL. This is not in fact necessary. The degree to which strong feelings of this kind are desirable is questionable, and in any case is (at least for our present purposes) more a matter of mental health than moral education. The person with PHIL must feel sufficiently to act on his belief in equality, but need not feel more. Thus it is sufficient if an older boy thinks that a nervous new boy needs some help (rather than dismissing him because he is a new boy, stupid, too young to bother about, etc.) and actually helps him: it is not required that the older boy himself goes through (or has earlier gone through) parallel agonies of nervousness.

3. It is important to realise what is meant by "other *people*". It is not in virtue of their having two legs or one head that we think human beings to have rights and to be equals. Rather it is because they have desires, wants, feelings, and purposes: they are conscious and (to a greater or lesser degree) intelligent and rational. (A religious person might put this

[2] See below under EMP and GIG.

by saying that they have souls.) This distinguishes human beings from the lower animals, plants, and physical objects. The importance of this point is that many people, consciously or unconsciously, seem to assume that some other criterion is what really counts—e.g. whether they have white skins, or speak English, or come from a similar social class, or are members of the same gang. Our criterion would enable us to include all "people" (even if from another planet and with tentacles instead of arms!)[1]

4. Similarly it should be clear what is meant by regarding other people as *equals*. We do not of course mean that a person should consider other people to be equally clever, heavy, rich, etc., as himself: they may be more or less so. We mean rather that he should recognise their equality of status as moral and conscious beings, each of whose wills and desires count as much as his own. It is in this sense that "all men are equal" points to an important truth.[2]

5. It is not required that a person should consider another person as *more* important than himself: only as of *equal* importance. He should not be afraid to stand up for his rights, or to make his own wants and interests felt. Of course it is possible that he may *prefer* to abandon his own immediate interests for the sake of another; indeed in so far as a person can genuinely feel unselfish and loving it is to be expected that this will happen. But we should beware of pseudo-unselfishness and pseudo-altruism here. Genuine altruism involves a further stage of moral education which goes beyond justice and equality: it is not entailed by what we mean here by PHIL. (See also 2(b) above.)

Dimensions in PHIL

6. We may distinguish two important dimensions in PHIL:

(a) *Scope*. This is, roughly, *how many* other people a person is prepared to include in his attitude of respect or equality. Thus some will show PHIL only for people of the same age-group, in the same gang, of the same race, etc.: others will extend it more widely.

(b) *Degree*. This is *not* (see 2(b) above) the intensity of feeling which a person has, but roughly how often or how consistently a person shows PHIL within whatever range his PHIL oper-

ates. Thus if a person shows PHIL towards (say) members of the same gang, there is still a question about how often he does so: his PHIL may operate 100% of the time within this range, or at a lower degree.

Questions for PHIL

Does the pupil even *say* that all other human beings have rights of equal importance with his own? Or does he consciously believe that coloured people, Jews, those of a different social class, etc., really are "inferior"?

If he says he believes in equality, is he *just* saying it, or does he really *mean* it? Is he just paying lip-service to a fashionable way of thinking, or does he really believe it?

If he does believe it, does he show forth this belief in his behaviour? Does he really *adopt* the attitude of PHIL?

How does he actually *treat* certain people (whom perhaps he might look down on, or be unreasonably in awe of): e.g. nervous new boys, pupils of the opposite sex, authority-figures, coloured people, etc.). Does he treat them as equals or not?

Does he listen to their opinions and allow them to have their say? If he and his group are deciding what to do, does he allow what *they* want to count? Or does he dismiss what they want as unimportant?

If a quite different kind of person from those he is used to comes within his experience—a foreigner, for instance, or somebody whose social behaviour is very unlike his own—does he regard him as an "outsider", or does he accept him as equal with himself even though his behaviour is different?

Does he make some *effort* to find out what other people's wants and feelings actually are, however good or bad his ability to discern this (EMP) may be?

EMP

What is EMP?

EMP is an *ability*, not a feeling or an attitude. Concern for other people—the general feeling or attitude that their interests count—is PHIL: EMP is simply the ability to know what other people are feeling, in particular situations. Rough definitions

[1] On this point C. S. Lewis's *Out of the Silent Planet* is illuminating.
[2] See John Wilson, *Equality* (Hutchinson, 1966).

3

might be "awareness of other people's feelings", "insight", or "the ability to understand what people's interests are", "knowledge of human emotions, desires, etc.". EMP must not be confused with *sympathy*, which is not an ability but a feeling.

1. The ability of EMP is thus something which may, at least in principle, be disjoined from PHIL. It is possible for someone to know what others are feeling, or would be likely to feel, with a very high degree of awareness or insight, and yet not to *care* about them. (A dictator who was very good at manipulating other people's emotions for his own selfish ends would be an example.)

2. Since EMP is an ability and not a behavioural trait, it is possible for a person to have a high degree of EMP and yet not actually to *use* this ability very much in practice. For instance, he may be very nervous about people, and hence too frightened to observe them closely in everyday life: or he may be lazy, and not bother: nevertheless he may still have the ability to tell what other people are feeling, and if only he was not nervous or lazy he would use it. (Of course if he *is* and always has been nervous or lazy about other people, he will probably not in fact have developed very much EMP: but the distinction is still an important one.)

3. EMP is concerned not only with awareness of the feelings of people with whom one actually comes into contact in one's everyday life: it includes also being able to predict the feelings of those whom one has never met—people in other countries, in the future, in the past, and so on.

4. By "other people's *feelings*" we are not primarily concerned with sensations but with emotions and desires. These can be detected in human beings in the following ways:

(a) By what a person *says* he feels: e.g. "I'm frightened".
(b) By characteristic *symptoms*: e.g. trembling at the knees, sweating, etc.
(c) By characteristic *action*: e.g. running away from the danger.
(d) By characteristic *circumstances*: e.g. dangerous things.

The person with a high degree of EMP will know about all these, in the case of all the human emotions, and also be able to correlate them. Thus he will know that stammering and turning pale are characteristic symptoms of nervousness or anxiety: he will also know what the person with these symptoms is likely to say and do, and he will have some idea about what circumstances are making him nervous. All

these are ideally required if someone is to have full and proper knowledge of another person's feelings.

Dimensions in EMP

5. These are much the same as for PHIL. To repeat them briefly:

(a) *Scope*. How *many* of other people's feelings he has the ability to be aware of.
(b) *Degree*. How precise and profound his awareness of those feelings is.

Questions for EMP

Can the pupil give a reasonably good account of the feelings of (say) a new boy at the school, or his own teacher, or his classmates in particular situations?

Does he find it difficult or easy to understand why, in school and outside it, different people behave as they do?

Does he find this difficult or easy with reference to people in past history? With reference to characters in plays or novels?

Can he act or play the rôle of other people effectively (someone being bullied, a foreigner arriving in a strange country, a criminal, etc.)?

Has he a fair idea of what is meant by the words which stand for people's feelings ("jealousy", "anxiety", "aggression", "love", etc.)?

Has he the ability to detect and be honest about *his own* feelings?

Has he the courage and emotional maturity to discuss his own feelings, whether or not he has the necessary vocabulary, skill in discussion, etc., to do so?

Whatever his ability, is he *interested* in other people's feelings and behaviour, or are his ideas about them based on no observation and thinking at all?

Is he competent at identifying and correlating what people say they feel, their symptoms, their behaviour, and the surrounding circumstances (see (4) above)?

GIG(1)

What is GIG(1)?

GIG(1) is perhaps the most easily describable of the components. It is an *attainment*: that is, we are here concerned with whether a person *actually knows* certain facts (not with whether he has the ability to learn them): namely those facts most relevant to moral situations.

1. The kind of facts relevant to GIG(1) are "hard" facts: not facts about people's feelings and desires, which come under EMP.

2. Plainly almost any such facts *might* be relevant to moral decisions: moreover, people in particular jobs or situations (e.g. doctors or lawyers) would be expected to know a great many more facts of a certain kind than other people would be expected to know. However, for practical purposes GIG(1) may be divided into two areas:

(a) Knowledge of the laws, rules and contracts of a person's society, and of the social system in general: also knowledge of conventions and social expectations.

(b) Knowledge of what things are dangerous to human beings in that society and elsewhere, including knowledge of relevant facts about the human body.

(These are repeated more fully below.)

3. In considering a person's GIG(1) we must (regrettably) resist the temptation to make allowance for his I.Q., home background, and so forth. We are simply interested in how many of the relevant facts a person knows. Whether or not it is his *fault*, if he knows very few facts, does not matter. Neither with GIG, nor with any of the other components, are we interested in assigning any particular kind of moral *blame* or *guilt*: only in establishing how far that person is morally educated.

Questions for GIG(1)

Does he have a reasonable knowledge of:

(a) The laws and rules enforced in his country and his local community (including the school), at least of those likely to affect him: and about the conventions and social expectations of his own and other social groups—what sort of manners are acceptable, what words and ritual phrases to use, how people react to certain kinds of dress, language, and behaviour, etc.? The general working of the society in which he finds himself?
The implicit or explicit contracts which operate in members of that society?

(b) What is dangerous and not dangerous to standard interests of other people—e.g. putting things on railway lines, excessively fast

driving, effects of certain drugs, etc.: also relevant facts in human biology and physiology—e.g. first aid, facts about pregnancy and other sexual matters, etc.?

GIG(2) (SOCIAL SKILLS)

What are Social Skills?

A person may possess and use the components so far listed—PHIL, EMP and GIG(1)—and yet fail to translate his moral decision into effective action. One reason for this may be that he lacks sufficient motivation, resolution or courage: this we shall consider under KRAT, our final component. But another reason may be that he lacks what we might call the "know-how". He might decide, for instance, to try to be nice to a new boy in a school and cheer him up: and he may be adequately motivated or resolved to put his decision into action: but he may not know *how to* be nice and cheer him up—perhaps he does not know just what words to use, or cannot speak to him without sounding patronising, and so forth. The general abilities required for effective action of this kind we shall call "social skills".

1. It must be recognised that "social skills" are not confined to group-situations, where (for instance) we might expect a person to be able to make the right sort of remarks at a party: they include abilities which are required for person-to-person behaviour as well. In this sense one might fail, e.g., to treat one's wife properly for lack of the relevant "social skill".

2. Social skills are of course closely connected in practice with EMP (knowledge of other people's feelings) and GIG (knowledge of facts, including facts about social norms and conventions). But the ability to act effectively towards other people demands more than this. The *kind* of knowledge is different: it is more like knowing how to swim, or how to play a particular game—not just a matter of knowing facts, but also a matter of being sufficiently practised and skilful to *perform* well. It is a kind of adeptness rather than a cognitive mastery of facts.

3. There are many different areas of social skills, depending on the context in which they are exercised. Thus the ability to discuss among equals is one thing: the ability to give orders is another: to take orders, yet another: and so on. We are chiefly interested here in those contexts and social relationships in which it is likely that most people will be called upon to perform: e.g., with groups of friends, as an employee, as a member of a committee, and so on.

5

Questions for GIG(1) (Social Skills)

> Is he capable of playing the rôles of a leader and a follower, of issuing and obeying instructions and orders?
>
> Can he behave efficiently in social situations involving (a) adults, (b) people much younger than himself?
>
> Can he behave well in formal or conventional contexts, and in less formal contexts?
>
> Can he discuss and debate effectively with his equals?
>
> Can he co-operate in decision-making, e.g. on a committee?
>
> Does he put other people at their ease in social situations?
>
> Does he in general use language adequately in social situations?

DIK

What is DIK?

DIK is best described as a *mode of thought*. A person with a high degree of DIK, when he faces up to a moral situation (various kinds of failure to face up to such situations may be caused by lack of KRAT), will consider that situation primarily in terms of other people's interests. He will bring the appropriate attitude (PHIL), his ability to discern other people's feelings (EMP), and his knowledge of "hard" facts (GIG), to bear on that situation: and as a result he will make a prescriptive moral choice, dictated by other people's interests, which he regards as committing him and anyone else in a similar situation to *action*. Such a person will normally have a number of *moral principles*, which he has arrived at in this way.

1. It is not required, of course, that a person should go through this procedure every time he is faced with a moral situation. A reasonable person should already have formulated at least some moral principles or generalisations, and have the settled habit of acting on them without too much thought. But a person with DIK would be able, if asked, to give at least some indication of *why* he behaved as he did—however habitual or unplanned his action was: and his reasons would relate to other people's interests. *Mere* habit is not enough: it has to be habit generated by an earlier process of moral reasoning, of the kind described.

2. It is assumed that the notion of "having a moral principle" or "making a moral choice" carries with it the notion of *universalisability*: that is, a person who makes such a choice does not make it for himself alone or for that situation only. Moral choices are of the form "I—and anyone else in the same position—ought to do so-and-so": or to put it another way, of the form "*One* ought", not just "I" or "you" or "He ought". This is important, because morality is a matter of prescribing what is right for human beings in general to do. For instance, if I think myself morally entitled to make as much money as possible, or to defraud my business partner, then I must logically think that other people have this right, and that my business partner can defraud me.

3. It is also assumed that moral choices are *overriding*. That is, the person who says "I ought to do so-and-so" has to mean more than just that he thinks it right, in a mild way, that he should do it—with the implication that, if things become difficult or he is going to suffer for it, then it would no longer be the right thing to do. He has got to think that it is *the* right thing for him to do in that situation, not just something which it would be nice to do in principle.

Dimensions of DIK

DIK is a complex moral component, but the two most important dimensions may be described briefly as follows:

(a) *Right reasons.* Not everybody makes, or even thinks he ought to make, his moral decisions on the basis of other people's interests. Other modes of thought besides DIK are regrettably common. Amongst these are: obedience to authority, conformity to what one's social group thinks or expects, guilt-feelings, uncritical obedience to rules, a tendency to do what is most expedient for oneself, following one's immediate impulses, and just having a vague and unrationalised feeling that something is right or wrong. Nearly everybody uses some one or other non-DIK mode of thought in *some* area of moral choice (sexual behaviour is a good example). The person with a high degree of DIK will always consider other people's interests, and think in this mode rather than in others.

(b) *Sincerity of decision.* There are also people who may pay lip-service to a certain mode of moral thinking (whether DIK or some other), and say that certain things would be right or wrong, but who do not sincerely *commit* themselves in making these judgements. They may call something "good" or say that one "ought" to do it, but they may not use these words in a way which really *prescribes action on their part*. (For instance, they may just mean by "good" "what is commonly supposed to be good".) The person with DIK will not just evaluate moral situations by reference to other people's interests, but actually make his moral *choices* and decisions, and commit himself, by reference to those interests.

Questions for DIK

Does he think that morals are "just a matter of taste", "all relative", etc., or does he believe that there are right and wrong answers to moral questions?

Does he think that other people's interests are what *ought* to count in a moral situation, or does he think that moral questions should be settled by other means (obeying an authority, avoiding a sense of guilt or shame, doing what everybody else does, doing what pays, etc.)?

If he does believe in taking other people's interests into account, does he actually do this in his moral thinking, or does he in fact follow some other criterion (what authority tells him, sense of guilt, etc.)?

Does he make use of whatever PHIL, EMP and GIG he has for his moral decisions?

When he uses words like "good", "bad", "right", "wrong", "ought", etc., does he use them in such a way as really to commit himself to acting in a certain way, or does he just mean "what other people (perhaps just adults) *think* is good" (. . . "right", etc.): i.e. to what extent does he really have a *prescriptive* moral vocabulary at all?

When he makes moral judgements, does he really believe that they apply to *all* people in similar situations, including himself (universalisability?)

Does he have a reasonably coherent set of moral principles—not necessarily completely fixed and certain, but at any rate seriously held for obvious cases (murder, stealing, lying, etc.)?

Do his principles include not only avoiding bad actions, but doing good ones (not only not

harming other people, but actively and positively helping them)?

KRAT(1) AND (2)

What is KRAT?

All the previous components—PHIL, EMP, GIG, and DIK—are all components of moral *thinking*: an attitude, an ability, an attainment, a mode of thought and other abilities. KRAT is quite different. Here we are concerned with *action* or *behaviour*. Anything that is required over and above the other components for rational moral action and behaviour will come under the heading of KRAT. Something like "behavioural traits necessary for morality" might serve as a partial definition: however, it is plain enough that KRAT does not stand for any one thing, but rather for an assortment of things any or all of which may be required for appropriate moral behaviour.

1. KRAT-traits enter into a person's moral thought and action in two basic ways.

   (a) A person must have the alertness and sensitivity actually to *use* the other components in his moral thinking, as opposed to having the abilities, etc., but not actually using them (KRAT(1)).
   (b) When a person has reached a rational moral decision, he must have the motivation and resolution to translate that decision into action (KRAT(2)).

2. It is a mistake to think of KRAT simply in terms of willpower. There are all sorts of reasons why people fail to bring their abilities to bear on moral situations, or fail to translate their moral decisions into action. They may be forgetful, incompetent, lazy, frightened, tired, cowardly, etc.: and not all of these are what would normally be called *moral* failures.

3. The complexities of KRAT are very considerable, and the best we can do here is to list some generalised KRAT-traits that seem of particular importance:

   (a) A person should have a sufficient *sentiment* or *love* for other people: this is at least *one* kind of motivation which should enable him both to think and act rationally in the moral sphere.
   (b) A person should have "good habits", or a settled disposition to think and act in a rational

SUMMARY. LIST OF COMPONENTS

Name	Status	Rough definition	Details
PHIL	Attitude	Regarding others as equals, taking their interests as equally important.	(i) Scope (how many "others") (ii) Degree (how firm/consistent the attitude)
EMP	Ability	Ability to know what others are feeling, and what their interests are.	(i) Scope (how many "others") (ii) Degree (amount and precision of knowledge)
GIG (1)	Attainment	Knowledge of "hard" facts relevant to moral choices.	(i) Law, contracts and social norms (ii) Danger, safety, human biology, etc.
GIG (2) (Social Skills)	Ability	Practical "know-how" to perform effectively in social contexts.	
DIK	Mode of thought	Ability to prescribe action for oneself for right reasons.	(i) Rightness of reasons (ii) Sincerity of decision
KRAT (1) and (2)	Motivation and behavioural traits	Factors required (a) to use the other components, (b) to translate consequent moral judgement into action.	(i) Alertness (ii) Resolution

manner: also seem well motivated. One cannot perhaps feel sentiment towards other people all the time, and this kind of motivation seems of very great practical importance.

(c) A person must possess independence of judgement, the ability to think and act autonomously (as opposed simply to following other people like sheep), and sufficient courage to act on his judgement; this seems a necessary quality, since there will be plenty of cases where rational morality goes against what is publicly acceptable.

(d) A person must be reflective or thoughtful enough not to be carried away by particular situations, and not to be forgetful of other people. He needs fixed habits, but he also must be able to stop and think when required. He needs, as it were, some kind of warning system which operates in him and tells him to think about what he is doing before he does anything.

Questions for KRAT

Does he *feel* strongly and favourably enough towards other people for him to be adequately motivated in thinking morally and in actually carrying out his moral principles?

Does he have good and settled habits which enable him to translate his moral principles into action without difficulty?

Does he have sufficient independence of judgement or "conscience" to make up his own mind and act in moral situations, regardless of what other people think?

Does he have sufficient sensitivity for situations involving other people to stop and think before acting?

C. Assessment in Other Terms

We hope that the investigator will find it reasonably practicable to refer his curricular analysis to the moral components: but nothing prevents him from using the analysis to assess other aims, or other factors, which may be relevant to moral education. Two types of phenomena are important here:

1. *Indicators.* Although the morally educated person cannot be properly defined except by reference to the components, many features *may* be good *indicators* of whether pupils are likely to possess some of the components or not. For instance, such phenomena as the delinquency rate of a class or a school, the amount of bullying, or even voluntary contributions to charity or social work, may be good guides to the components.

2. *Preconditions.* Again, there are certainly a number of factors which, though not themselves moral components, may be essential prerequisites or preconditions for a person's being able to develop the components. Thus the ability to make friends, or to express oneself verbally, or to be reasonably free from anxiety, may be important preconditions in this sense.

Of course it is rash to claim that we know with anything like certainty just which *are* the right indicators and preconditions. But there is no harm, and might be much good, in an attempt to assess the curriculum in terms of this sort, as well as in terms of components. Hence the investigator might like to add some of these in the assessment-column (column G) of his charts.

We would, however, strongly advise the investigator to steer clear of trying to assess the morally educated person in terms which are much more vague than the terms of the components themselves. Such words and phrases as "sensitivity", "maturity", "responsibility", "decent behaviour", "getting on with other people", and so forth will not suitably or profitably figure in the assessment-column. In so far as these terms are clear at all, they seem to stand for multiple abilities and attitudes, which need to be broken down into their component parts if we are to make any solid progress. Anything which the investigator wishes to add in the assessment-column, then, must above all be clearly defined and in principle readily identifiable.

MODEL*

Column A Titles	Column B Contents		Column C Methods		Column D Contexts	
Subjects: History English Biology etc.	*Rote learning* *Facts and descriptions:* "Hard" About people	☐ ☐ ☐	*Sources of learning:* Teacher Group work Own research	 ☐ ☐ ☐	*Type of communication:* Coherent Incoherent Authoritarian Liberal Co-operative	 ☐ ☐ ☐ ☐ ☐
	Deductive thinking	☐	*Tools of learning:* Books Newspapers	 ☐ ☐	Competitive	☐
Topics/areas: R.K. Sex General studies Social studies etc.	*Inductive thinking:* "Hard" About people *Value judgements:* Moral Prudential Concepts and language Aesthetic appreciation *Self-expression and skills:* Discussion and debate Acting and rôle-playing Creative skills Physical skills (others to be added)	 ☐ ☐ ☐ ☐ ☐ ☐ ☐ ☐ ☐ ☐	Own observation Films TV *Demanded product:* Homework Essays Diaries or scrap-books Contributions to discussion *Testing and exams:* Public exams Classroom tests Marks for group work, etc. (others to be added)	☐ ☐ ☐ ☐ ☐ ☐ ☐ ☐ ☐ ☐	*Topography and other* *arrangements:* In school Outside school Rows of desks Grouped informally Food or drink *Teacher's personality:* "Subject"-orientated Pupil-orientated Authoritarian Liberal Male Female	 ☐ ☐ ☐ ☐ ☐ ☐ ☐ ☐ ☐ ☐ ☐
NOTES	NOTES		NOTES		*Social class:* Same as pupils Higher than pupils Lower than pupils Young-looking Old-looking Experienced Inexperienced Committed Uncommitted Extrovert Introvert *Size of class:* over 35 20–35 under 20 (others to be added)	 ☐ ☐ ☐ ☐ ☐ ☐ ☐ ☐ ☐ ☐ ☐ ☐ ☐ ☐
					NOTES	

*In order to help assessment, further blank copies of

1

Column E Time	Column F Pupils	Column G Assessment		
			1st ass.	*2nd ass.*
☐ periods of	*Social class and home background:*	PHIL		
☐ minutes each, for	Upper ☐	(scope and degree)	☐	☐
☐ days each week, for	Upper-middle ☐	EMP		
☐ weeks	Middle ☐	(scope and degree)	☐	☐
	Lower-middle ☐	GIG (1)		
Total:	Lower ☐	Law and social norms	☐	☐
☐ hours	Stable homes ☐	Danger, safety, biology	☐	☐
	Unstable homes ☐	GIG (2)		
NOTES	Cultured homes ☐	(Social Skills)	☐	☐
	Uncultured homes ☐	DIK		
		(right reasons and		
	Peer-groups relationships:	sincere decisions)	☐	☐
	In a gang ☐	KRAT (1) and (2)		
	Not in a gang ☐	Alertness	☐	☐
	Committed as "teenager" ☐	Resolution	☐	☐
	Not so committed ☐	Indicators and preconditions to be added		
	Member of youth club ☐	(see pp. 8–9)		
	Sex:	NOTES		
	Only boys ☐			
	Only girls ☐			
	Mixed ☐			
	Average age ☐			
	Area of school intake:			
	Rural ☐			
	Urban ☐			
	Suburban ☐			
	Mixed ☐			
	Intelligence and verbal ability:			
	intelligence			
	very good ☐			
	good ☐			
	average ☐			
	poor ☐			
	very poor ☐			
	verbal ability			
	very good ☐			
	good ☐			
	average ☐			
	poor ☐			
	very poor ☐			
	(others to be added)			
		TIME ELAPSED		
		between 1st and 2nd assessment:		
	NOTES	☐ week(s) ☐ month(s) ☐ year(s)		

the model have been provided at the end of this volume.

CHAPTER 2

Analysis of the Curriculum

In Model 1, on pp. 10–11, our analysis of the curriculum is divided into seven parts. These must be dealt with in turn.

A. Titles

The investigator might well start with simply looking at the *titles* given to various periods taught in the curriculum, as in column A. He will find that these titles suggest a very mixed bag of subjects and topics. On the one hand, there will be titles that stand for what at least seem to be clearly-defined and recognisable subjects—"Latin", "History", "English literature", and so on: on the other hand, there will be titles for periods which leave the actual *content* of such periods very loosely defined, if indeed they are defined at all. Thus a title like "Religious knowledge" gives no very clear indication of what is actually taught: and titles such as "Man and his environment", "Our neighbours", or "General studies" give hardly any indication at all.

For purposes of convenience, we may make a rough distinction between (1) title of *subjects or disciplines,* and (2) titles of *topics or areas of study.*[1] (1) will include those titles which give us a fairly clear idea of the contents: that is, of what special skills, forms of thought, and kinds of knowledge the pupil will be expected to deploy. One rough test would be whether we would have a fairly good idea of how to examine a pupil in the subject. Such titles would be "Arithmetic", "Spelling", or "Biology": we might also include, though with a bit more hesitation, such titles as "History" and "English literature". (2) will include the vaguer titles like "R.K.", "Social studies" or "General studies".

The investigator will remember, of course, that since his interest is in moral education he need not list all the titles of all periods. Only those which he thinks might be relevant to moral education need be dealt with. However, if he is in any doubt about including a title, he should err on the side of safety and include it in the list. One obvious reason for this is that a title might bear very little relation to its contents: for instance, a title like "French" may look wholly irrelevant to moral education, but if it turns out that the French master spends a lot of time discussing the differences between French and English people, or moral problems in contemporary France, it would plainly be extremely relevant. Another reason is that the social interaction that occurs during all periods, whatever their contents, may be very important. We assume here that the investigator will have at least sufficient knowledge of what actually happens in the period to form a sound preliminary judgement about what titles to include.

B. Contents

We now turn to column B in Model 1, where the investigator is required to specify the contents that are actually taught under these titles. This is of crucial importance, but it is also one of the hardest tasks which the investigator faces. We are here concerned with the question of what exactly it is that the pupils are given to *learn*. With such subjects and disciplines as Latin, Mathematics and History there is perhaps less difficulty in answering this question.[1]

---

[1] On this distinction, and on the curriculum generally, see *Introduction to Moral Education*, pp. 406 *et seq.*; my article "Orthodox, General or Integrated?" in *Universities Quarterly*, Sept. 1967; Paul Hirst's "Liberal Education and the Nature of Knowledge", in R. D. Archambault's collection *Philosophical Analysis and Education* (Routledge), and Paul Hirst's *Philosophical Foundations of the Curriculum* (Routledge).

[1] Though even here there are problems. When we say "Latin", do we mean the ability to translate Latin authors, or compose from English into Latin, or understand the culture of the ancient Romans? When we set out to teach "History", are we chiefly concerned that the pupil knows the dates of the kings of England, or do we want him to know how to use a historical source, or do we want him to have some idea of his

But when it comes to areas like "Sex" or "Getting on with one's classmates" the difficulties are considerable. With "Sex", are we interested in handing out biological information, or helping them to understand the psychology of the opposite sex, or getting them to realise the social problems of sex, or what? Does "Man and his environment" mean history, or contemporary literature, or sociology, or some kind of science? Is "R.K." a matter of indoctrinating belief, or teaching facts about the Bible, or discussing moral problems?

The crucial point here, so far as an investigation of school practice is concerned, is not whether the headmaster or other authority gives one answer rather than another. What *ought* to be incorporated in the teaching of such areas is a very open question, and one on which this Research Unit can certainly not pronounce. The point is that *some clear answer* must be given. For if it is not, the investigator can have no clear view of what actually goes on in the curricular periods labelled "Sex", or "General studies", or "R.K.". It is much more important, at this stage, to have a clear view of what actually does go on, rather than worry too much about whether something different ought not to go on: or more precisely, our worries are likely to be fruitless unless and until we have a clear view to begin with.

Note here that we are concerned with what *actually* happens, rather than with what is *intended* to happen. This is important for two reasons. First, what is intended to happen may be very different from what actually happens: for instance, it may be the headmaster's intentions that the pupils should learn something about the spirit of Christianity in a R.K. class: but in fact the teacher may teach in such a way that all the pupils are given is a few facts about the Bible and the journeys of St. Paul. Or, again, a headmaster may wish to induce *concern* about the problems of old people: but the actual discussion may do no more than try to give the children some *facts* about the numbers of old people, their average income, and so on. Secondly, the school authorities may have no clear intentions at all about what is supposed to happen. They may be quite uncertain about what ought to happen in periods about "Sex" or "Religion": indeed they may never have raised the question at all.

This has, however, also to be distinguished from

own and his country's place in history, or what? It's no good talking about *methods* of teaching even these subjects unless we're first clear what we *mean* by them, and what sort of aims we have under such vague headings as "Teaching History" or "Learning Latin". Many contemporary studies of "new methods" in teaching subjects are vitiated by this lack of clarity.

how far the teaching and learning are *successful*. Thus in the example of R.K. teaching above, we must distinguish:

(a) The intention of the school authorities, or of the actual class-teacher (to acquire an inner understanding of the Christian spirit).
(b) The kind of teaching the children are actually *given* (only historical facts, dates, to know passages of the Bible by heart).
(c) Whether the children learn more or less successfully from that teaching (they may not actually *learn* many historical facts, dates, etc.).

Our concern is with (b). At the initial stages of investigation we are interested in *what (logical) kinds of teaching go on*. This means we are looking at whether the children are given facts, or taught how to think, or taught certain skills—we are concerned with the logically different types of teaching or education.

Our interest here corresponds, then, to the general question "*What* are the pupils being taught?": as opposed to our interest in column C, which is (roughly) "By what *methods*?" and column D, which is "In what *context*?". The important thing to remember is that the "What" in our question is not the same as "*About* what". Pupils can be taught *about* sex: but this still leaves it open whether they are taught biological facts, awareness of other people's feelings, appreciation of comparative sexual *mores* in various countries, or whatever. We are concerned not with the subject-*matter* but with the *kinds* of things taught. Again, "English literature" can be taught simply as a series of dates and facts about English authors, or with the intention of increasing the pupil's awareness of particular poems and plays. Both of these are cases of teaching *about* "English literature": but they are plainly very different: and it is these differences, rather than differences in the subject-matter, which are the important ones.

This is, of course, a very complex topic: and the investigator cannot be expected to give any very precise or detailed account of the particular skills or modes of thought which are being taught. Nevertheless, he should be able to make at least the basic distinctions in terms of which the items in column B are set out. Some illustration of these may be helpful here.[1]

[1] It may be of interest to add that this kind of analysis should be found useful not only for moral education, but for other areas of education as well: in particular, perhaps, for some of the new areas of study being developed in many schools. I am thinking here of areas often entitled "Integrated studies", "General studies", "Environmental studies", and so forth.

1. *Rote learning.* A self-explanatory category: examples would be of children taught to recite the multiplication tables, or pieces of poetry, or grammatical rules, by heart. Of course such learning may relate importantly to other categories, but it may nevertheless be considered in itself.
2. *Facts and descriptions.* These may be (a) "hard" facts about the physical world, such as we teach in science: (b) facts about *people.* (b) may include, for instance, general descriptions of the social practices and personal feelings in past societies, or in other societies than our own in the present day. Much of what could be called "psychology", "sociology", or "anthropology" comes under this heading, as well as history. Facts about other people's feelings would be particularly relevant to one moral component (EMP): and these may be taught under many titles (history, R.K., etc.).[1]
3. *Deductive thinking.* The model example here is mathematics: others would be the application of the rules of grammar, or the rules of certain games. Here the child is not taught so much to *observe* the outside world and think about it, but rather to apply axioms and rules so as to get the right answer.[2]
4. *Inductive thinking.* This again divides into (a) thinking about "hard" (scientific) facts, tracing causal connections in the world, understanding and testing scientific theories and being able to give scientific explanations: and (b) thinking on the basis of facts about people—being able to explain and understand why people do things, what their feelings and motives are likely to be in certain situations, and so on (a good deal of history is concerned with this). This also includes the use of imagination in such thinking.
5. *Making value-judgements* (moral and prudential). This is taught whenever the children are asked to consider, in some more or less coherent way, what is *good* or *right*, or what a person *ought* to do: either (a) in reference to other people (a moral judgement), or (b) in

reference only to his own life and happiness (prudential). The way in which moral judgements are or ought to be made has already been outlined in the last chapter.[1] Thus the pupil may be asked to consider whether Henry V was a good king or a bad king: whether rich people ought to pay more income tax: whether one ought to go to the dentist regularly, and so on.
6. *Concepts and language.* This is taught in a great many ways. There is a sense, of course, in which learning any subject involves understanding the use of concepts (for instance, the concept of multiplication in mathematics, or the concept of gravity in science): but we are here concerned with more direct instruction. This will occur for the most part in learning to read and widen one's vocabulary: in the study of languages and literature: and in the study of the *meaning* of concepts (philosophy).
7. *Aesthetic appreciation.* This includes such things as the proper enjoyment of and awareness of the qualities found in music, painting, poetry, and so forth: it must be distinguished from (i) "hard" facts about the dates of authors, the technical facts of music, etc., and (ii) developing awareness of other people's feelings. (Both of these, as well as aesthetic appreciation, may come into the study of literature.)
8. *Self-expression and skills.* This includes such things as learning to discuss and debate, how to act a part in a play, how to play the piano or perform effectively in the swimming-pool or on the hockey field. It will be found that most of what is not included in the first seven categories above will come under this heading.

It must not be thought that these categories are either wholly distinct from each other, or a complete list. The investigator will do well to use them as far as possible: but he may find that he has to make up more categories of his own—or at the very least to make some additional notes about the contents of particular periods, rather than just assign a tick or a cross to each of these eight headings. They are intended only as a general guide.

C. Methods

Here again the investigator must use his own judgement, since it is difficult to make a complete

---

[1] Biology of course deals with "facts about people", but should nevertheless come under (a): for biological facts are "hard" or scientific facts. By "facts about people" we mean here facts about what they feel, intend, desire, like and dislike, etc., and their social practices rather than their physical make-up.

[2] This is inserted chiefly to make the list reasonably complete: it is not expected that much instruction of this kind is *directly* relevant to moral education, though it may be of indirect importance.

[1] pages 1–9.

14

list of every single method that a teacher might use. In column C we have divided the possible methods under four general headings, and most methods should be able to find a place under one or the other of these.

1. *Sources of learning*. Here we want to know *from* whom, and by what *general* methods, the children are supposed to learn. Thus one teacher may spend most of the time dictating notes to the children: another may encourage them to do most of the work themselves, and to learn by looking things up in books: another may get children in a group to work in common on a project: another involve the children in discussions, social surveys, rôle-playing, and so forth.

2. *Tools of learning*. We are concerned here with the actual objects or "hardware" of learning. Does the teacher use books? How about visual aids—films, wall-charts, closed-circuit TV? Any question of this kind should be answered under this heading.

3. *Demanded product*. This is a matter of what the teacher *expects to get* from his pupils: thus, some teachers will demand a great deal of written work, whereas others may be content with an occasional essay or a few short notes. Are the children expected to contribute to classroom discussion? Are they given homework? Are they supposed to keep diaries or scrapbooks? This sort of question is relevant here.

4. *Testing and exams*. Closely connected with 3, this is concerned with how (if at all) a subject is assessed or "examined". We put "examined" in inverted commas, because this is not just a question of whether the teaching is related to any public examination (like the G.C.E. or the C.S.E.), though of course this is one important thing to look out for. But the investigator must also see whether there are formal or informal tests given to the pupils, any marking system, or any way by which the pupils know that they have done well or badly: and if so, of what sort they are.

Investigators are again reminded that this list is not complete, and that they should themselves supplement it by a full account.

D. Contexts

It will not be easy for the investigator to distinguish these altogether from the methods: but what follows about the items under this general category may help to make this plain.

1. *Type of communication*. Here we want to know what sort of thing is going on in the classroom (or wherever the learning takes place)—what kind of "social interaction" is taking place both amongst the children, and between the children and the teacher. We may say generally that we are interested in the *psychological* and *sociological* features of the teaching situation, and perhaps the two dimensions most significant here are (a) whether the situation is coherent and purposeful, or incoherent and chaotic: (b) whether it is dominated by the teacher in an "authoritarian" way, or is shared more liberally by teacher and pupils working on a more equal basis: (c) whether it is co-operative or competitive. Under (a)—what we have called the "coherent–incoherent" dimension— we should ask "Is it a situation where the teacher just gives orders, and the children are supposed to obey them? Or is it a situation where teacher and pupil are more on an equality?" Under (b)— the "authoritarian–liberal" dimension—we might ask: "Is there a very strict discipline imposed by a set of rules, or is there a natural discipline imposed by the interest of the subject, or is there chaos?" The important features here can be observed by noting who does most of the talking, who is listened to most, who takes the initiative, and so on. Under (c) we want to know how far the children work co-operatively in groups or pairs, and how far each individual child is encouraged to compete with his neighbours rather than helping them or being helped by them.

2. *Topographical and other arrangements*. Here we want to know where the learning occurs, and under what physical conditions and arrangements. Questions here would be (a) "Is it in school or outside? If in school, in what sort of room? Do the pupils have their own formroom? If outside, where does it happen? In a museum where the pupils wander round looking at things, or in a slum street where they do social surveys, or in one of the staff's private house?" (b) "Are the children behind their desks in rows, or in a circle? Where does the teacher sit? Are the chairs comfortable? Is food and drink (e.g. coffee) provided?"

3. *Teacher's personality*. Here we are chiefly concerned with deploying a few of the more important distinctions that might be made on

this topic. We ask, for instance, whether the teacher is "subject-orientated" or "pupil-orientated": whether he is "authoritarian" or "liberal": male or female: young-looking or old-looking: of the same social class and background or different: committed to a particular religion or metaphysic (Christianity, Marxism, etc.) or uncommitted: extrovert or introvert: experienced or inexperienced. We should also want to know his position in the school (it may make a difference if he is the headmaster), and anything else about him that might seem of particular significance to his pupils (e.g. if he wears a clerical collar, or has won a V.C. in the war: if she is foreign or coloured, or wears the latest fashionable clothes).

4. *Size of class.* Self-explanatory.

E. Amount of Time Spent

This category is straightforward: we want to know only how *much* teaching, in terms of time simply, is given under the title in column A, in the ways described in the other columns: e.g. 2 hours a week for 36 weeks a year. Of course we must break this down. Thus it is not sufficient to know that so many hours are spent on (say) "History": we need to know more specifically how much time is spent on particular content-types (column B) that might feature under the title of "History"—roughly x hours on learning dates and "hard" facts, y hours on learning to think about how people in past societies viewed the world, z hours on making moral judgements about historical figures, and so on. Similarly we need to assess, at least roughly, the amount of time spent using certain methods (column C) and spent in particular contexts (column D). This may best be done, however, by assigning percentages to the items in columns B, C and D (see A.3, below (p. 17)), which the investigator may find easier than giving a great many time-assessments in column E (one for each content-type, method, context, etc.).

We are, of course, concerned here with a "before-and-after" study: that is, with an attempt to see if children in a certain class are more morally educated *after* they have been given certain kinds of teaching than they were *before* (see pp. 10–11). So our interest in the amount of time spent will be partly dictated by how long a period we intend to leave between the "before" and the "after". This must depend on the investigator's own judgement: but it is obvious that, in trying to judge how far curricular

subjects affect the development of moral components, one must allow a reasonable length of time factor. Further, a course on English literature which lasts for a couple of weeks will, very probably, have a quite different effect from one which lasts for a whole year: moreover, the effect may be different in kind as well as in degree. To quote an example from my own experience, I found when teaching philosophy to schoolboys that the first term's work (for two periods a week) had little if any effect, either on the pupils' moral education or (so it appeared) on anything else: but that after the first term it began to pay very good dividends. Not till then did they catch on to the idea of the subject, develop a real interest in it, and put it to good use in their everyday life and thinking. The same may well apply to other subjects.

Probably a full term is a minimum length of time during which to allow for the investigation: a year would be a good deal better. In any case, once the investigator has decided how much time he wants to elapse between "before" and "after", he can then fill in column E. What he puts here, of course, will not be the length of real elapsed time between "before" and "after", but the actual amount of man-hours for which the children have been taught. Thus for a year's elapsed time, the man-hours of a particular R.K. class might be one period of 45 minutes, for four days a week, for 36 weeks (i.e. a whole school year): total time spent, 108 hours.

F. Pupils Taught

Naturally it may be the case that particular contents, methods and contexts will work for certain types of pupils, but not for others. So we need some rough-and-ready assessment of pupil-types, for which the following may serve as a basis:

1. *Social class and home background.* This is best considered in terms of (a) father's profession; income; education of father and mother; living conditions (type of housing); newspapers taken; TV programmes watched; books in the home, and so on. This merges into (b), where we are more concerned with the psychological situation at home: amount of communication between parents and child; whether the parents get on well with each other, or are divorced or separated; whether both parents are living; what kinds of friends the parents encourage; whether the child has brothers and sisters, and so on.

2. *Peer-group relationships.* What sort of friends does the pupil have? Is he a member of a gang? What sort of gang? How do he and his friends spend their time? How does he/she get on with the opposite sex? Does he belong to any youth club or other organisation? How far is he committed to the rôle of a "teenager"? These are some of the relevant questions here.

3. *Sex.* Quite simply, whether the pupils taught are boys, girls, or mixed.

4. *Age.* Self-explanatory.

5. *Area of school intake.* It may be important to know whether the school catchment area is a rural one, or urban: what kind of jobs are available: how much time the pupils spend in large towns, or in the country, or in the suburbs, and so forth.

6. *Intelligence and verbal ability.* To some extent self-explanatory: but the investigator should try to take into account the natural aptitudes and latent abilities of the pupils which may not be brought out by an I.Q. test. In particular he should pay attention to the verbal ability of the pupils, using this phrase in a wide sense. This is not so much a matter of mere breadth of vocabulary, but the ability to think and talk in a logically sophisticated manner (rather than merely using clichés, short phrases and sentences, etc.).

PROCEDURE

When the investigator has thoroughly mastered the above, and understood Model 1, we should suggest that he should now proceed as follows:

A. Preliminary

First equip yourself with a large number of big sheets of paper, on which to carry out the investigations suggested by Model 1, and a notebook.

1. Start by making a list of *titles.* For each title, take a number of *instances.* Probably this will take the form of a title, (1) as taught by Mr. X, (2) as taught by Miss Y, and so forth. So you will need a number of sheets of paper for each title. These might be headed, for instance, "RELIGIOUS KNOWLEDGE" (Mr. X's class), or "ENGLISH LITERATURE" (Miss Y's class), and so on. How many instances you will be able to take under each title naturally depends on your time and resources: but you ought ideally to take at least several instances of each title. For the

chances are that it is not in what titles are taught that the relevant factors can be found, but rather in the kind of components, methods, contexts or teacher's personality that are deployed.

2. Next, decide on how long a time you are going to allow to elapse between the start and the finish of the investigation of each particular instance. For example, you might decide to look at Instance 1: RELIGIOUS KNOWLEDGE (Mr. X's class) over the period of a school year. Then, for purposes of comparison, you would probably decide to look at Instance 2: RELIGIOUS KNOWLEDGE (Miss Y's class) over the period of a year also. (On the question of what time to allow, see above, p. 16, under E.) You should now have a master-sheet which would perhaps look something like this:

RELIGIOUS KNOWLEDGE	Instance 1 Mr. X's class	one year
	Instance 2 Miss Y's class	one year
SEX	Instance 1 Mr. L's class	two terms
	Instance 2 Mr. M's class	two terms
	Instance 3 Miss O's class	two terms
ENGLISH LITERATURE	Instance 1 Mr. P's class	one year
	Instance 2 Miss Q's class	one year
	Instance 3 Miss R's class	one year

and so on.

3. Now you will also have a lot of separate sheets of paper, one sheet for each instance. For example, the sheet which is to deal with RELIGIOUS KNOWLEDGE Instance 1 above will have that heading, and look as shown in Model 2. Now you can get going.

B. First Assessment

1. Take the first of your sheets, and look at column G. Here the moral components are listed. Add to these any aims of your own or of the school which seem to be relevant to moral education.

2. Now use the assessment-methods suggested in Chapter 1 (pp. 1–11), and make a rough assessment of the pupils in the class-periods which you are going to analyse. If you can do this for individual pupils as well as for the class as a whole, so much the better: in that case you will need as many columns as the number of pupils or groups of pupils you are going to assess. But you may have to be content with assessing the general average of the class, in respect to the moral components.

3. In any case, put down some figure in the sub-column headed "First Assessment" in column G. Since the purpose of the exercise is to discover, after you have done the analysis, whether the children

Column B Contents		Column C Methods		Column D Contexts	
Rote learning	☐	*Sources of learning:*		*Type of communication:*	
		Teacher	☐	Coherent	☐
Facts and descriptions:		Group work	☐	Incoherent	☐
"Hard"	☐	Own research	☐	Authoritarian	☐
About people	☐			Liberal	☐
		Tools of learning:		Competitive	☐
Deductive thinking	☐	Books	☐	Co-operative	☐
		Newspapers, etc.	☐		
Inductive thinking:		Own observation	☐	*Topography and other*	
"Hard"	☐	Films	☐	*arrangements:*	
About people	☐	TV	☐	In school	☐
				Outside school	☐
Value-judgements:		*Demanded product:*		Rows of desks	☐
Moral	☐	Homework	☐	Grouped informally	☐
Prudential	☐	Essays	☐	Food or drink	☐
Concepts and language	☐	Diaries or scrap-books	☐		
Aesthetic appreciation	☐	Contributions to discussion	☐	*Teacher's personality:*	
				"Subject"-orientated	☐
Self-expression and skills:		*Testing and exams:*		Pupil-orientated	☐
Discussion and debate	☐	Public exams	☐	Authoritarian	☐
Acting and rôle-playing	☐	Classroom tests	☐	Liberal	☐
Creative skills	☐	Marks for group work, etc.	☐	Male	
Physical skills	☐	(others to be added)		Female	☐
(others to be added)					

NOTES	NOTES	

		Social class:	
		Same as pupils	☐
		Higher	☐
		Lower	☐
		Young-looking	☐
		Old-looking	☐
		Experienced	☐
		Inexperienced	☐
		Committed	☐
		Uncommitted	☐
		Extrovert	☐
		Introvert	☐
		Size of class:	
		over 35	☐
		20–35	☐
		under 20	☐
		(others to be added)	

NOTES

2

KNOWLEDGE

1

class)

Column E Time	Column F Pupils	Column G Assessment		

☐ periods per day,
of
☐ minutes each,
for
☐ days each week,
for
☐ weeks
Total:
☐ hours
 	
NOTES
	*Social class and
	home background:*
	Upper ☐
	Upper-middle ☐
	Middle ☐
	Lower-middle ☐
	Lower ☐
	Stable homes ☐
	Unstable homes ☐
	Cultured homes ☐
	Uncultured homes ☐
	
	Peer-group relationships:
	In a gang ☐
	Not in a gang ☐
	Committed as "teenager" ☐
	Not so committed ☐
	Member of youth club ☐
	
	Sex:
	Only boys ☐
	Only girls ☐
	Mixed ☐
	Average age ☐
	
	Area of school intake:
	Rural ☐
	Urban ☐
	Suburban ☐
	Mixed ☐
	
	Intelligence and verbal ability:
	intelligence
	  very good ☐
	  good ☐
	  average ☐
	  poor ☐
	  very poor ☐
	verbal ability
	  very good ☐
	  good ☐
	  average ☐
	  poor ☐
	  very poor ☐
	  (others to be added)
	
	NOTES
			1st ass.	*2nd ass.*

		PHIL (scope and degree)	☐	☐
		EMP (scope and degree)	☐	☐
		GIG (1)		
		Law and social norms	☐	☐
		Danger, safety, biology	☐	☐
		GIG (2)		
		(Social Skills)	☐	☐
		DIK (right reasons and sincere decisions)	☐	☐
		KRAT (1) and (2)		
		Alertness	☐	☐
		Resolution	☐	☐
		Indicators and preconditions to be added (see pp. 8–9)		
		NOTES		
		TIME ELAPSED between 1st and 2nd assessment: ☐ week(s) ☐ month(s) ☐ year(s)		

have improved in respect of each of the moral components, it does not greatly matter in what kind of way you score the "First Assessment" column: almost any mark will do, so long as you remember what it stands for. An easy way would be to assign a mark out of 10. But you must have some fairly clear idea, however you note it in this column, of how the children stand in respect of each component: for without this, you will not be able to say after the analysis whether they have benefited or not.

4. You may find it very difficult to mark all the components and aims. Try your best: but if it is impossible, it will still be useful to write some general description, e.g. "a very rude and noisy class", or "this class contains a lot of delinquents", or "people in this class are always breaking school rules", or something of that kind. Any assessment is better than none.

C. Analysis

1. Keep hold of your first sheet, and make a kind of preliminary reconnaissance of the items in columns B, C, D, E, and F. You may add to these lists at this stage (before the actual investigation) if it seems that important items have been omitted from the model: but perhaps it might be better to make these additions in the course of the investigation itself, when you will be more easily able to observe important features that have been left out.

2. Next, have a look at the actual periods taught for your first "instance" (e.g. R.K. in Mr. X's class). Tick those items in column B which seem to be true of these periods, mark with a cross those items which do not seem to be true. If some features are partly or occasionally operative, you may tick them and also assign percentages or scores to them: for instance, if Mr. X spends most of the time teaching "hard" facts, but some of the time in discussion of moral problems, then you might want to put "Hard" facts, 85%: making value-judgements, 15%.

3. Now do the same for columns C, D, E, and F.

4. In the course of doing this, you will find the rather over-simplified features listed in the various columns inadequate, so that the ticks and crosses put against them fail to convey the truth of the situation. It may be (a) that you need extra features on the list (as suggested in (2) above), or (b) that the terms used to describe the features are not entirely adequate. This will certainly be the case with column F. Here you need to add notes of your own about the situation. It is best to do these, so far as possible, in

terms of Model 1—by amplifying the features on it, and giving further explanations of what you find in the teaching-periods.

5. Now do the same for another "instance", and then for other titles and instances on your master sheet.

D. Second Assessment

You should now have a great many sheets of paper, arranged in a number of piles, with each pile corresponding to a title, and the pile consisting of the various instances of that title which you have analysed. Now comes the crucial stage of the second assessment. Deal with each sheet as follows:

1. First, look at column G. Here the moral components are listed. Add to these any aims of your own or of the school which seems to be relevant to moral education.[1] Write all the items in column G into your own sheets, if you have not already done so.

2. Now use the assessment-methods suggested in Chapter 1 (pp. 1–11), and try to determine by those or any other method whether the teaching as analysed by you on *each sheet*, actually seems to develop any of these moral components, or fulfil any of the aims. Here you must try to discover whether *individual children*, as well as the class or group as a whole, have benefited or not.

3. If your view is that all or most of the children have benefited in one respect or another, it will be easiest to put a tick against that moral component or aim in respect of which you think they have benefited: and a cross against the others. You may leave blank, or put a query, against those components or aims where you are quite uncertain.

4. You may find, however, that some children have benefited and some have not. Here perhaps the best thing to do is to put a tick, but also an asterisk referring to your own additional notes concerning which children have benefited and which have not.

5. Finally, fill in the time elapsed, between your first and second assessment, in the bottom right-hand corner.

E. Conclusions

1. When you have decided all this, you will then be able to see more clearly what it is about these

[1] On this see the Introduction, pp. vii–ix.

teaching-periods that are or may be responsible for this development. You will be able to say something like: "Such-and-such a title, with such-and-such contents, taught by such-and-such methods, in such-and-such a context, by such-and-such a teacher, for so many hours, to pupils of such-and-such a kind, seems to achieve aims P, Q, or R, or develop components X, Y, and Z": and, by contrast, you may see that other methods, contexts, etc., fail to develop these or any other aims or components. This should enable you to pin down more exactly where the relevant factors are. It may be, for instance, that the teacher's personality seems to count for more than the title: or that the context is more important than the content: and so on. By checking your assessment against the ticks and crosses you have made in the various columns, and referring to your own notes, this should become reasonably clear. You should write a brief report on this.

2. Either at this stage or, if you prefer, before beginning the second *assessment* (D above) at all (not of course before doing the *analysis* (C above)), you may try to see in what ways the curricular practice of the school is self-contradictory. (Thus if in one instance children are encouraged to discuss, talk to the teacher as equals, etc., and in another they are forced to remain silent and obey orders, this looks as if there was a kind of contradiction.) It would be wise to write a brief report on this also.

EXAMPLE. It may help to clarify this procedure if we take an example.

Suppose you decide to begin by investigating the instruction given about sex, in curricular periods with that title. You might decide to take two instances of this, so that you will start with two sheets of paper which look like the example given above of Religious Knowledge: only in this case the first will be headed SEX: Instance 1 (as taught by Mr. Smith), and the second SEX: Instance 2 (as taught by Miss Brown). Suppose they both have classes in this for one 45-minute period, 4 days a week, for a school year.

Start with Instance 1 and go through the procedure above. Do the "first assessment", in column G. Write in, if you haven't already done so, any other aims that seem relevant (perhaps "avoidance of sexual offences coming before the juvenile courts"). Then do the analysis. In Instance 1, you may find that Mr. Smith spends most of the time teaching them the "hard" facts of biology, a bit of time in discussion, and a bit of time on encouraging the children to make moral judgements: that his methods mostly consist of dictating notes, getting the children to look up things in the dictionary, and that he uses

no visual aids: that he does this only in the classroom, with the children sitting in rows behind the desks: that he is a fairly authoritarian personality: that his classes occur twice a week for a whole academic year: and that his pupils come from working-class homes, are both boys and girls aged about 15, etc. So your sheet of paper for Instance 1 will now be full up, except for the second assessment in column G.

Now you conduct the second assessment. You try to find whether the pupils taught by Mr. Smith have improved in respect of any moral component or any aim. Suppose you conclude that most of the pupils' factual knowledge (GIG) has improved, and that some of the boys' awareness of other people's feelings (EMP) has improved, but that otherwise there has been no improvement. Finally, fill in the elapsed time. Then your completed sheet will end up looking like Model 3.

You now look at SEX: Instance 2 (as taught by Miss Brown). Do the first assessment in column G: and we will suppose that this looks much like that of Instance 1. But in the analysis, suppose you find very different material. Miss Brown spends far more time in discussion, encourages the children to express themselves and learn other people's feelings, uses visual aids, takes the children out to talk to people outside the school, and is non-authoritarian, or "liberal", in her general approach. Suppose also that she teaches children of essentially the same kind.

Now you make the second assessment: and suppose you find that the children have not improved as regards factual knowledge (GIG), but that they have all improved in awareness of other people's feelings (EMP), and that some boys have improved in respect for other people (PHIL) and in forming reasonable moral principles (DIK). You may find also that their general behaviour is more efficiently motivated, and that to some extent they put their moral principles into action better, by having more courage to act in accordance with what they think to be right (KRAT). Fill in the elapsed time. Then your completed sheet will look as in Model 4.

What you induce from this is, of course, an open question. But at least you know that Miss Brown's periods produce what appear to be better results, and that the relevant factors are likely to lie somewhere in the difference of content, methods, context, etc., which you have ticked and crossed in columns B, C, and D—since the data in columns E and F is similar for both Miss Brown and Mr. Smith. Of course there will be many differences between Mr. Smith's and Miss Brown's periods, so that it is not clear which of the differences are relevant and which

MODEL

Instance

(Mr. Smith's

Column B Contents		Column C Methods		Column D Contexts	
Rote learning	✓	*Sources of learning:*		*Type of communication:*	
		Teacher	✓	Coherent	✓
Facts and descriptions:		Group work	✗	Incoherent	✗
"Hard"	✓ (80%)	Own research	✗	Authoritarian	✓
About people	✗			Liberal	✗
Deductive thinking	✗	*Tools of learning:*		Competitive	✓
		Books	✓	Co-operative	✗
Inductive thinking:		Newspapers, etc.	✓*		
"Hard"	✓	Own observation	✗	*Topography and other*	
About people	✗	Films	✗	*arrangements:*	
		TV	✗	In school	✓
Value-judgements:				Outside school	✗
Moral	✓*	*Demanded product:*		Rows of desks	✓
Prudential	✓	Homework	✓	Grouped informally	✗
Concepts and language	✗	Essays	✓	Food or drink	✗
Aesthetic appreciation	✗	Diaries or scrap-books	✗		
		Contributions to discussion	✗	*Teacher's personality:*	
Self-expression and skills:				"Subject"-orientated	✓
Discussion and debate	✓ (59%)	*Testing and exams:*		Pupil-orientated	✗
Acting and rôle-playing	✗	Public exams	✗	Authoritarian	✓
Creative skills	✗	Classroom tests	✓	Liberal	✗
Physical skills	✗	Marks for group work, etc.	✗	Male	✓
(others to be added)		(others to be added)		Female	✗

NOTES	NOTES	
* Moral judgements made on Christian dogmatic basis.	* Only "respectable" papers encouraged (*Times, Telegraph,* etc.)	

Social class:

Higher than pupils	✓
Same	✗
Lower	✗
Young-looking	✗
Old-looking	✓
Experienced	✓
Inexperienced	✗
Committed	✓
Uncommitted	✗
Extrovert	✓
Introvert	✗

Size of class:

over 35	☐
20–35	☐
under 20	☐
(others to be added)	

NOTES

3 SEX

1

class)

Column E Time	Column F Pupils	Column G Assessment		
[1] period(s) per day, of [45] minutes each, for [4] days each week, for [36] weeks *Total:* ([93] hours	*Social class and home background:* Upper [X] Upper-middle [X] Middle [X] Lower-middle [✓] Lower [X] Stable homes [✓] Unstable homes [X] Cultured homes [X] Uncultured homes [✓]			
		PHIL (scope and degree)	*1st ass.* [3]	*2nd ass.* [X]
		EMP (scope and degree)	[3]	[✓]*
		GIG (1)		
		Law and social norms	[2]	[X]
		Danger, safety, biology	[2]	[✓]
		GIG (2)		
		(Social Skills)	[3]	[X]
		DIK		
		(right reasons and sincere decisions)	[2]	[X]
		KRAT (1) and (2)		
		Resolution	[5]	[X]
		Alertness	[3]	[X]
NOTES	*Peer-group relationships:* In a gang [✓] Not in a gang [X] Committed as "teenager" [✓] Not so committed [X] Member of youth club [X]	Indicators and preconditions to be added (see pp. 8–9)		
	Sex: Only boys [X] Only girls [X] Mixed [✓]* Average age [15]	NOTES * Boys only.		
	Area of school intake: Rural [X] Urban [✓] Suburban [X] Mixed [X]			

	Intelligence and verbal ability:
	intelligence
	  very good [X]
	  good [X]
	  average [✓]
	  poor [X]
	  very poor [X]
	verbal ability
	  very good [X]
	  good [X]
	  average [X]
	  poor [✓]
	  very poor [X]
	(others to be added)			

	NOTES * But mostly boys.	TIME ELAPSED between 1st and 2nd assessment: [1] week(s) [10] month(s) [ ] year(s)		

MODEL

Instance

(Miss Brown's

Column B Contents		Column C Methods		Column D Contexts	
Rote learning	✗	*Sources of learning:*		*Type of communication:*	
		Teacher	✓ (10%)	Coherent	✓
Facts and descriptions:		Group work	✓ (50%)	Incoherent	✗
"Hard"	✓ (10%)	Own research	✓ (40%)	Authoritarian	✗
About people	✓ (0%)			Liberal	✓
		Tools of learning:		Competitive	✗
Deductive thinking	✗	Books	✗	Co-operative	✓
		Newspapers, etc.	✗		
Inductive thinking:		Own observation	✓	*Topography and other*	
"Hard"	✗	Films	✓	*arrangements:*	
About people	✓	TV	✓	In school	✓
				Outside school	✓
Value-judgements:		*Demanded product:*		Rows of desks	✗
Moral	✓ *	Homework	✗	Grouped informally	✓ *
Prudential	✓	Essays	✗	Food and drink	✓
Concepts and language	✗	Diaries or scrap-books	✓		
Aesthetic appreciation	✗	Contributions to		*Teacher's personality:*	
		discussion	✓	"Subject"-orientated	✗
Self-expression and skills				Pupil-orientated	✓
Discussion and debate	✓	*Testing and exams:*		Authoritarian	✗
Acting and rôle-playing	✓	Public exams	✗	Liberal	✓
Creative skills	✗	Classroom tests	✗	Male	✗
Physical skills	✗	Marks for group		Female	✓
(others to be added)		work, etc.	✓		
		(others to be added)		*Social class:*	
				Higher than pupils	✓
				Same	✗
				Lower	✗
				Young-looking	✓
				Old-looking	✗
				Experienced	✗
				Inexperienced	✓
				Committed	✓
				Uncommitted	✗
				Extrovert	✓
				Introvert	✗
				Size of class:	
				over 35	✗
				20–35	✓
				under 20	✗
				(others to be added)	

NOTES

Column B:
* Moral judgements made on basis of other people's interests.

Column C:
NOTES

Column D:
NOTES
* Sometimes in the teacher's own home, sitting informally and having coffee.

4 SEX

1

class)

Column E Time	Column F Pupils		Column G Assessment		
[1] period(s) per day, of [45] minutes each, for [4] days each week, for [36] weeks *Total:* [108] hours	*Social class and* *home background:*		PHIL	*1st ass.*	*2nd ass.*
	Upper	☒	(scope and degree)	[3]	☑*
	Upper-middle	☒	EMP		
	Middle	☒	(scope and degree)	[4]	☑
	Lower-middle	☑	GIG (1)		
	Lower	☒	Law and social norms	[2]	☒
	Stable homes	☑	Danger, safety, biology	[2]	☒
	Unstable homes	☒	GIG (2)		
	Cultured homes	☒	(Social Skills)	[3]	[3]
	Uncultured homes	☑	DIK		
			(right reasons and		
NOTES	*Peer-group relationships:*		sincere decisions)	[2]	☑*
	In a gang	☑	KRAT (1) and (2)		
	Not in a gang	☒	Alertness	[5]	☑
	Committed as "teenager"	☑	Resolution	[3]	[1]
	Not so committed	☒	Indicators and preconditions to be added		
	Member of youth club	☒	(see pp. 8–9)		
	Sex:				
			NOTES		
	Only boys	☒	* Boys only.		
	Only girls	☒/			
	Mixed	☑*			
	Average age	[15]			
	Area of school intake:				
	Rural	☑			
	Urban	☒			
	Suburban	☒			
	Mixed	☒			
	Intelligence and verbal ability:				
	intelligence				
	very good	☒			
	good	☒			
	average	☑			
	poor	☒			
	very poor	☒			
	verbal ability				
	very good	☒			
	good	☒			
	average	☒			
	poor	☑			
	very poor	☒			
	(others to be added)				
			TIME ELAPSED		
	NOTES		between 1st and 2nd assessment:		
	*But mostly boys.		[1] week(s) [10] month(s) ☐ year(s)		

are unimportant. But if you took a third instance, where there were only a few differences, you might be able to narrow it down still further. Thus if Mr. Smythe does almost everything that Mr. Smith does, but uses films and other visual aids which Mr. Smith does not, and yet gets results more like those of Miss Brown, that would suggest the visual aids to be one very important factor.

It will be seen that the research task here can be extended indefinitely, in an endeavour to pinpoint the really important factors. We do not imagine that very many readers will be in a position to devote enormous amounts of time and energy to this, and the investigator will inevitably have to proceed to some extent on an intuitive basis. Thus an imaginative observer, after his analysis and assessment of the two instances above, may be able to guess that the relevant factors are the visual aids, or perhaps the differences between Mr. Smith and Miss Brown as personalities, or the fact that Miss Brown uses discussion-methods more than Mr. Smith, or whatever. If he can arrange that the school tries out new practices (with different teachers, contents, methods, etc.), he may gain a still clearer idea of what is important.[1]

You have also to remember that the changes that occur, as marked in your assessment, over the time elapsed *may* not be caused at all by anything to do with the curricular periods. They may be due to the social context of the school, or the natural development of the children, or their experiences outside the school. There are a great many possibilities here, which you can try to take into account: but you must not expect to achieve anything like *certain* knowledge of why the children have developed. Research in this field is not as easy as that. But you may well, by a combination of luck, judgement and a judicious use of the procedure here outlined, produce some extremely useful findings.

SOME FURTHER QUESTIONS

The pace of educational change is very rapid: and the very notion of "the curriculum", "subjects", "periods", etc., are in the melting-pot. But not all change, however fashionable, is for the better. Certainly we must be eager and enthusiastic to try out new ideas: but our analysis of the curriculum will already have shown the need for thinking clearly, and in appropriate categories, about what exactly it is that we are doing—whether new or old.

[1] Of course this example is not a real one, and may be quite implausible: it is used only as an illustration.

If we do not do this, we are likely to fall into one or both of two errors. Suppose we try out a new idea X, and appear to get a certain result Y. Thus X might be "discussing sex", and Y might be "the pupils are very interested". Then (1) we don't know what it is about X that produces Y: is it the subject, or the fact that there is discussion, or the personality of the teacher, or merely that it is a new idea? (2) we don't know whether Y is a *good* result unless we are much clearer about how it actually affects the children. Thus children and adolescents may indeed be very interested in sex, but this does not necessarily mean that they *learn* anything. In other words, without being clear about X we don't know *what* it is that produces a "hit" or a "miss": and without being clear about Y we don't know whether it actually *is* a "hit" or a "miss".

After using the analytic models, the teacher or other investigator may still feel uncertain about what changes to make in the curriculum. It may be hard for him to generalise his findings—to be able to say, in plain English, just what new ideas are likely to work and why. To some extent this difficulty is inherent in the research-topic itself: we cannot indeed be certain without a lot more work. However, there is quite a lot of evidence (partly from the social sciences, and partly from the experiences of practising teachers) about which general factors are likely to be important; so I shall conclude by directing the reader's attention to these factors, simply by asking a series of questions. These must not be allowed to prejudice the use of the analytic models, which the investigator should already have used for himself, and drawn his own conclusions: but they may nevertheless be of some help.[1]

A. The Curriculum in General

Some of the relevant points here were made in the Introduction (pp. vii–ix). Questions here are: How much time do you want the pupils to spend on what could be called curricular periods, as against informal social experiences inside and outside the school? What sorts of things do you think can be taught formally, and what sorts of things have to be picked up informally? How much of "moral education" can be done by the curriculum? Can the curriculum be extended so as to do more in this direction? Are you sure that the informal, non-curricular contexts will do the job, if the curriculum cannot?

[1] For a discussion of these see *Introduction to Moral Education*, pp. 403–13.

B. Content

Here we can make our questions a bit more precise:

1. Is it clear, to the teacher *and* to the children, just what disciplines and skills are supposed to be learnt in particular periods? Do the pupils know what counts as success, as "getting it right"?
2. Are the periods sufficiently concerned with the pupils' *own emotions*, or are they more to do with "external" facts (about old people, war, local government, etc.)?
3. Is there some attempt to teach the pupils those basic *skills* and *approaches* for which the academic titles "philosophy", "sociology" and so forth stand? (Some teachers would feel themselves ill-equipped for these approaches, and some would fear that they are too abstract for their pupils. But in practice there are forms of "pre-philosophical", "pre-sociological", etc., thinking which schoolboys and schoolgirls respond to very well.)
4. Are there any periods which make a *direct* attempt to teach the "moral components" (PHIL, EMP, DIK, etc.)?
5. Are there periods designed to increase the pupil's verbal ability, in oral as well as written work?
6. Are there periods involving mime, drama and impromptu acting and rôle-playing? Do these help the non-verbal pupil in particular?
7. Are those problems which the pupils meet in their homes and peer-groups dealt with?

C. Method

1. Are the pupils taught to learn on their own initiative (by using libraries, making social surveys, etc.)?
2. Is the reality of the subject brought home to the pupils by film-loops, tape-recordings, etc.?
3. Are the visual aids supported by discussion?
4. Is there some clear testing- or assessment-system whereby the pupils can know what sort of progress they have made?

D. Context

1. How well does team-teaching work? Does the pupil need to have *one permanent* teacher with whom he can identify and feel secure?
2. How does the teacher handle the feelings his pupils have for him, be they affectionate or hostile? Is he warm enough, but also sufficiently uninvolved? Does he feel threatened by close relationships with the pupils?
3. Do the children spend enough time in learning-contexts *outside* the school?
4. Are the class-rooms (however modern) too bleak, or are they warm and "cosy" enough? Do the pupils play a part in being responsible for the rooms, and altering them?
5. Are the disciplinary "ground rules" laid down with complete clarity, and efficiently enforced?
6. Are different arrangements used for different types of learning: e.g. sitting round a table or in a circle for joint discussions, sitting in rows for "lectures", and so forth?
7. Can the teacher play the different rôles that are required ("lecturing" as an authority, discussing as an equal, etc.)?

In the present state of research in this field, it is not certain that these are necessarily the most relevant or important questions. To some of them teachers may very well answer "Maybe yes, maybe no, it doesn't matter two pins either way." But research must always proceed by asking too many questions, and then in the light of the evidence selecting the most important.

It may well be that there are other questions, not asked here, which teachers will want to pose, exploring other classes of factors of great importance. Here too only the evidence, as it comes in, can help us to judge.

In either case, the need of the moment is to go out with questions, and come back with answers: and evidence for the answers must be as "hard" as it is possible to make it.

Postscript

As both this guide and our first publication will have made plain, it is essential (in this of all topics) that research and practical experience should go hand in hand. All research workers must rely, to a very great extent, on the findings and experience of those who are not themselves full-time researchers. Only thus will the research workers be able to feed back practical and useful suggestions into the main stream of educational practice.

For this reason, we of the Farmington Trust Research Unit would be extremely grateful if those who make any serious use of this book would let us know about their findings. As we are only a small unit, it will be appreciated that we shall not necessarily have time to enter into a great deal of correspondence about them: but that does not diminish their importance.

Any information should be addressed to:

The Director,
  Farmington Trust Research Unit,
    4 Park Town,
    Oxford.
      (Telephone: Oxford 57456 and 56357.)

Column A Titles	Column B Contents	Column C Methods	Column D Contexts
Subjects: History English Biology etc. *Topics/areas:* R.K. Sex General studies Social studies etc.	*Rote learning* ☐ *Facts and descriptions:* "Hard" ☐ About people ☐ *Deductive thinking* ☐ *Inductive thinking:* "Hard" ☐ About people ☐ *Value judgements:* Moral ☐ Prudential ☐ Concepts and language ☐ Aesthetic appreciation ☐ *Self-expression and skills:* Discussion and debate ☐ Acting and rôle-playing ☐ Creative skills ☐ Physical skills ☐ (others to be added)	*Sources of learning:* Teacher ☐ Group work ☐ Own research ☐ *Tools of learning:* Books ☐ Newspapers ☐ Own observation ☐ Films ☐ TV ☐ *Demanded product:* Homework ☐ Essays ☐ Diaries or scrap-books ☐ Contributions to discussion ☐ *Testing and exams:* Public exams ☐ Classroom tests ☐ Marks for group work, etc. ☐ (others to be added)	*Type of communication:* Coherent ☐ Incoherent ☐ Authoritarian ☐ Liberal ☐ Co-operative ☐ Competitive ☐ *Topography and other* *arrangements:* In school ☐ Outside school ☐ Rows of desks ☐ Grouped informally ☐ Food or drink ☐ *Teacher's personality:* "Subject"-orientated ☐ Pupil-orientated ☐ Authoritarian ☐ Liberal ☐ Male ☐ Female ☐ *Social class:* Same as pupils ☐ Higher than pupils ☐ Lower than pupils ☐ Young-looking ☐ Old-looking ☐ Experienced ☐ Inexperienced ☐ Committed ☐ Uncommitted ☐ Extrovert ☐ Introvert ☐ *Size of class:* over 35 ☐ 20–35 ☐ under 20 ☐ (others to be added)
NOTES	NOTES	NOTES	NOTES

1

Column E Time	Column F Pupils	Column G Assessment

<table>
<tr><td colspan="2">

☐ periods of
☐ minutes each, for
☐ days each week, for
☐ weeks

Total:
☐ hours

NOTES

</td><td colspan="2">

Social class and home background:
Upper ☐
Upper-middle ☐
Middle ☐
Lower-middle ☐
Lower ☐
Stable homes ☐
Unstable homes ☐
Cultured homes ☐
Uncultured homes ☐

Peer-groups relationships:
In a gang ☐
Not in a gang ☐
Committed as "teenager" ☐
Not so committed ☐
Member of youth club ☐

Sex:
Only boys ☐
Only girls ☐
Mixed ☐
Average age ☐

Area of school intake:
Rural ☐
Urban ☐
Suburban ☐
Mixed ☐

Intelligence and verbal ability:
intelligence
  very good ☐
  good ☐
  average ☐
  poor ☐
  very poor ☐
verbal ability
  very good ☐
  good ☐
  average ☐
  poor ☐
  very poor ☐
(others to be added)

NOTES

</td></tr>
</table>

Column G – Assessment

	1st ass.	*2nd ass.*
PHIL (scope and degree)	☐	☐
EMP (scope and degree)	☐	☐
GIG (1)		
Law and social norms	☐	☐
Danger, safety, biology	☐	☐
GIG (2)		
(Social Skills)	☐	☐
DIK (right reasons and sincere decisions)	☐	☐
KRAT (1) and (2)		
Alertness	☐	☐
Resolution	☐	☐

Indicators and preconditions to be added (see pp. 8–9)

NOTES

TIME ELAPSED
between 1st and 2nd assessment:
☐ week(s) ☐ month(s) ☐ year(s)

Column A Titles	Column B Contents	Column C Methods	Column D Contexts
Subjects: History English Biology etc. *Topics/areas:* R.K. Sex General studies Social studies etc.	*Rote learning* ☐ *Facts and descriptions:* "Hard" ☐ About people ☐ *Deductive thinking* ☐ *Inductive thinking:* "Hard" ☐ About people ☐ *Value judgements:* Moral ☐ Prudential ☐ Concepts and language ☐ Aesthetic appreciation ☐ *Self-expression and skills:* Discussion and debate ☐ Acting and rôle-playing ☐ Creative skills ☐ Physical skills ☐ (others to be added)	*Sources of learning:* Teacher ☐ Group work ☐ Own research ☐ *Tools of learning:* Books ☐ Newspapers ☐ Own observation ☐ Films ☐ TV ☐ *Demanded product:* Homework ☐ Essays ☐ Diaries or scrap-books ☐ Contributions to discussion ☐ *Testing and exams:* Public exams ☐ Classroom tests ☐ Marks for group work, etc. ☐ (others to be added)	*Type of communication:* Coherent ☐ Incoherent ☐ Authoritarian ☐ Liberal ☐ Co-operative ☐ Competitive ☐ *Topography and other arrangements:* In school ☐ Outside school ☐ Rows of desks ☐ Grouped informally ☐ Food or drink ☐ *Teacher's personality:* "Subject"-orientated ☐ Pupil-orientated ☐ Authoritarian ☐ Liberal ☐ Male ☐ Female ☐ *Social class:* Same as pupils ☐ Higher than pupils ☐ Lower than pupils ☐ Young-looking ☐ Old-looking ☐ Experienced ☐ Inexperienced ☐ Committed ☐ Uncommitted ☐ Extrovert ☐ Introvert ☐ *Size of class:* over 35 ☐ 20–35 ☐ under 20 ☐ (others to be added)
NOTES	NOTES	NOTES	NOTES

Column E Time	Column F Pupils	Column G Assessment

Column E — Time

- [ ] periods of
- [ ] minutes each, for
- [ ] days each week, for
- [ ] weeks

Total:
- [ ] hours

NOTES

Column F — Pupils

Social class and home background:
- Upper [ ]
- Upper-middle [ ]
- Middle [ ]
- Lower-middle [ ]
- Lower [ ]
- Stable homes [ ]
- Unstable homes [ ]
- Cultured homes [ ]
- Uncultured homes [ ]

Peer-groups relationships:
- In a gang [ ]
- Not in a gang [ ]
- Committed as "teenager" [ ]
- Not so committed [ ]
- Member of youth club [ ]

Sex:
- Only boys [ ]
- Only girls [ ]
- Mixed [ ]
- Average age [ ]

Area of school intake:
- Rural [ ]
- Urban [ ]
- Suburban [ ]
- Mixed [ ]

Intelligence and verbal ability:
intelligence
- very good [ ]
- good [ ]
- average [ ]
- poor [ ]
- very poor [ ]

verbal ability
- very good [ ]
- good [ ]
- average [ ]
- poor [ ]
- very poor [ ]

(others to be added)

NOTES

Column G — Assessment

	1st ass.	2nd ass.
PHIL (scope and degree)	[ ]	[ ]
EMP (scope and degree)	[ ]	[ ]
GIG (1) Law and social norms	[ ]	[ ]
Danger, safety, biology	[ ]	[ ]
GIG (2) (Social Skills)	[ ]	[ ]
DIK (right reasons and sincere decisions)	[ ]	[ ]
KRAT (1) and (2) Alertness	[ ]	[ ]
Resolution	[ ]	[ ]

Indicators and preconditions to be added (see pp. 8–9)

NOTES

TIME ELAPSED
between 1st and 2nd assessment:
- [ ] week(s)
- [ ] month(s)
- [ ] year(s)

Column A Titles	Column B Contents	Column C Methods	Column D Contexts

Subjects:
History
English
Biology
etc.
 	
Topics/areas:
R.K.
Sex
General studies
Social studies
etc.
	Rote learning ☐
	
	Facts and descriptions:
	"Hard" ☐
	About people ☐
	
	Deductive thinking ☐
	
	Inductive thinking:
	"Hard" ☐
	About people ☐
	
	Value judgements:
	Moral ☐
	Prudential ☐
	Concepts and language ☐
	Aesthetic appreciation ☐
	
	Self-expression and skills:
	Discussion and debate ☐
	Acting and
	rôle-playing ☐
	Creative skills ☐
	Physical skills ☐
	(others to be added)
		Sources of learning:
		Teacher ☐
		Group work ☐
		Own research ☐
		
		Tools of learning:
		Books ☐
		Newspapers ☐
		Own observation ☐
		Films ☐
		TV ☐
		
		Demanded product:
		Homework ☐
		Essays ☐
		Diaries or scrap-books ☐
		Contributions to
		discussion ☐
		
		Testing and exams:
		Public exams ☐
		Classroom tests ☐
		Marks for group
		work, etc. ☐
		(others to be added)
			Type of communication:
			Coherent ☐
			Incoherent ☐
			Authoritarian ☐
			Liberal ☐
			Co-operative ☐
			Competitive ☐
			
			Topography and other
			arrangements:
			In school ☐
			Outside school ☐
			Rows of desks ☐
			Grouped informally ☐
			Food or drink ☐
			
			Teacher's personality:
			"Subject"-orientated ☐
			Pupil-orientated ☐
			Authoritarian ☐
			Liberal ☐
			Male ☐
			Female ☐
			
			Social class:
			  Same as pupils ☐
			  Higher than pupils ☐
			  Lower than pupils ☐
			Young-looking ☐
			Old-looking ☐
			Experienced ☐
			Inexperienced ☐
			Committed ☐
			Uncommitted ☐
			Extrovert ☐
			Introvert ☐
			
			Size of class:
			  over 35 ☐
			  20–35 ☐
			  under 20 ☐
			  (others to be added)

NOTES	NOTES	NOTES	
			NOTES

Column E Time	Column F Pupils	Column G Assessment		
			1st ass.	*2nd ass.*
☐ periods of ☐ minutes each, for ☐ days each week, for ☐ weeks	*Social class and home background:* Upper ☐ Upper-middle ☐ Middle ☐ Lower-middle ☐ Lower ☐ Stable homes ☐ Unstable homes ☐ Cultured homes ☐ Uncultured homes ☐	PHIL (scope and degree) EMP (scope and degree) GIG (1) Law and social norms Danger, safety, biology GIG (2) (Social Skills)	☐ ☐ ☐ ☐ ☐	☐ ☐ ☐ ☐ ☐
Total: ☐ hours		DIK (right reasons and sincere decisions)	☐	☐
NOTES	*Peer-groups relationships:* In a gang ☐ Not in a gang ☐ Committed as "teenager" ☐ Not so committed ☐ Member of youth club ☐	KRAT (1) and (2) Alertness Resolution Indicators and preconditions to be added (see pp. 8–9)	 ☐ ☐	 ☐ ☐
	Sex: Only boys ☐ Only girls ☐ Mixed ☐ Average age ☐	NOTES		
	Area of school intake: Rural ☐ Urban ☐ Suburban ☐ Mixed ☐			

	Intelligence and verbal ability:
	intelligence
	  very good ☐
	  good ☐
	  average ☐
	  poor ☐
	  very poor ☐
	verbal ability
	  very good ☐
	  good ☐
	  average ☐
	  poor ☐
	  very poor ☐
	(others to be added)			

	NOTES	TIME ELAPSED between 1st and 2nd assessment: ☐ week(s) ☐ month(s) ☐ year(s)		

Column A Titles	Column B Contents	Column C Methods	Column D Contexts
Subjects: History English Biology etc. *Topics/areas:* R.K. Sex General studies Social studies etc.	*Rote learning* ☐ *Facts and descriptions:* "Hard" ☐ About people ☐ *Deductive thinking* ☐ *Inductive thinking:* "Hard" ☐ About people ☐ *Value judgements:* Moral ☐ Prudential ☐ Concepts and language ☐ Aesthetic appreciation ☐ *Self-expression and skills:* Discussion and debate ☐ Acting and rôle-playing ☐ Creative skills ☐ Physical skills ☐ (others to be added)	*Sources of learning:* Teacher ☐ Group work ☐ Own research ☐ *Tools of learning:* Books ☐ Newspapers ☐ Own observation ☐ Films ☐ TV ☐ *Demanded product:* Homework ☐ Essays ☐ Diaries or scrap-books ☐ Contributions to discussion ☐ *Testing and exams:* Public exams ☐ Classroom tests ☐ Marks for group work, etc. ☐ (others to be added)	*Type of communication:* Coherent ☐ Incoherent ☐ Authoritarian ☐ Liberal ☐ Co-operative ☐ Competitive ☐ *Topography and other* *arrangements:* In school ☐ Outside school ☐ Rows of desks ☐ Grouped informally ☐ Food or drink ☐ *Teacher's personality:* "Subject"-orientated ☐ Pupil-orientated ☐ Authoritarian ☐ Liberal ☐ Male ☐ Female ☐ *Social class:* Same as pupils ☐ Higher than pupils ☐ Lower than pupils ☐ Young-looking ☐ Old-looking ☐ Experienced ☐ Inexperienced ☐ Committed ☐ Uncommitted ☐ Extrovert ☐ Introvert ☐ *Size of class:* over 35 ☐ 20–35 ☐ under 20 ☐ (others to be added)
NOTES	NOTES	NOTES	NOTES

Column E Time	Column F Pupils	Column G Assessment		
			1st ass.	*2nd ass.*
☐ periods of	*Social class and home background:*	PHIL		
☐ minutes each, for	Upper ☐	(scope and degree)	☐	☐
☐ days each week, for	Upper-middle ☐	EMP		
☐ weeks	Middle ☐	(scope and degree)	☐	☐
	Lower-middle ☐	GIG (1)		
Total:	Lower ☐	Law and social norms	☐	☐
☐ hours	Stable homes ☐	Danger, safety, biology	☐	☐
	Unstable homes ☐	GIG (2)		
NOTES	Cultured homes ☐	(Social Skills)	☐	☐
	Uncultured homes ☐	DIK		
		(right reasons and		
	Peer-groups relationships:	sincere decisions)	☐	☐
	In a gang ☐	KRAT (1) and (2)		
	Not in a gang ☐	Alertness	☐	☐
	Committed as "teenager" ☐	Resolution	☐	☐
	Not so committed ☐	Indicators and preconditions to be added		
	Member of youth club ☐	(see pp. 8–9)		
	Sex:	NOTES		
	Only boys ☐			
	Only girls ☐			
	Mixed ☐			
	Average age ☐			
	Area of school intake:			
	Rural ☐			
	Urban ☐			
	Suburban ☐			
	Mixed ☐			
	Intelligence and verbal ability:			
	intelligence			
	very good ☐			
	good ☐			
	average ☐			
	poor ☐			
	very poor ☐			
	verbal ability			
	very good ☐			
	good ☐			
	average ☐			
	poor ☐			
	very poor ☐			
	(others to be added)			
		TIME ELAPSED		
	NOTES	between 1st and 2nd assessment:		
		☐ week(s) ☐ month(s) ☐ year(s)		

37